Post-Traumatic Poetry

poems by

Mackenzie Rose

Finishing Line Press
Georgetown, Kentucky

Post-Traumatic Poetry

ACKNOWLEDGMENTS

Immense appreciation for Emma Reed's winning oration of this collection at
the 2022 VHSL Forensics State Championship tournament.

Publisher: Leah Huete de Maines
Editor: Christen Kincaid
Cover Art: Mackenzie Rose
Author Photo: Patrick Elwell
Cover Design: Elizabeth Maines McCleavy

Order online: www.finishinglinepress.com
also available on amazon.com

Author inquiries and mail orders:
Finishing Line Press
PO Box 1626
Georgetown, Kentucky 40324
USA

Contents

*In endless gratitude to the Kentuckian angel
who gave me life twice*

Post-Traumatic Poetry

I can't put a screaming face
onto this page.

I can't place the vibrant orange-red
hue of splattered blood
between each word.

I can't produce the rubbery rawness
of the feeding tube
snaking down my throat, down
the book's spine.

I can't present the fear-gripped
muscles in each poem.

I can't portray what you want
to read
because I can't put a screaming face
onto this page.

To begin

Contrasting the opalescent snow
which illuminated annual Christmas trips,
the vernal hills undulated,
heaving and rolling, with May sunlight. Down I-81,
Roanoke beckoned,
and, within, entangled emotions
began to bubble.

By mid-morning, I was under
the campus's great White Oaks: a dewy
grass blade beneath their vast height.
The trailing hour held me
in anticipationanxietyangst against
the perfectly preserved
brick façades.

He drove separately, and his approach
baited the bubbling that filled my stomach,
spoiling it
into a sickness.

Hollins University became my favorite
destination; it represented a magic
that reality could never replicate.
Magic was scarce
in the routine world of 9-5s, "look
at your waistline,"
and always losing
that good hair tie.
So, I planted a White Oak deep inside
me for when I couldn't
taste the breakfast-lunch-dinner anymore.

But he arrived.
He held
two houseplants
in cheap terracotta pots
and found a brilliant white
lawn chair to occupy. His person evaporated
in the crowd, but his presence overwhelmed.
Standing to join the procession,
my graduating peers and I sweeped
the stage as ruddy-blush
swept my cheeks.

He held the two plants
without the sweet release of *congratulations*
that I expected.
My parents swarmed around me, he stood
drenched in self-isolation.

The sickness engulfed me,
rooting deep
into my stomach. The small seed of hope,
which I had only begun
to nurture, was ultimately trapped
and stunted for the next three years.

The roof line

lay
unprotected,
and I returned myself here
each day
to a hard jawline, to a stringent
smile, to him. The moths
in my stomach
stirred dust around, but never did I find
my butterflies. Unstable in the door,

the knob
fought to let me
inside, giving me a moment
to break free and find home
elsewhere. I never questioned
its assertiveness and simply entered

the cloud
of sunny haze
in which the dogs' hair twirled,
dipping in my wake
as I was beckoned

to the back. In the room,
he shared space
with the sweaty shoes
and construction materials;
he was another scrap of moulding
without a designation
in the house.

He poured guilt
around my feet like concrete. I stared
at the ceiling, thinking
of the roofline, the sharp
angle, the drop, but I was cemented

to the scratched
wooden floor without a way
to dig myself out.

Van over

The air lay
immobile within the vents.
  Hot
   yellow
    lines
     fled
      beneath the tires,
       silence pressed my lips. The sickening smell
of bicycle lube and ego, uncoiling
with the nostalgic flavor
of Hubba Bubba,
overwhelmed any sense of reasoning
or

happiness. I heard
my voice,

Don't you love

our little family?

It felt like an echo, pushed   back
to me, but he
     sat   rigid,
hands gripping the wheel with a frightening strength.
A wall occupying
that space. The highway
didn't stop; he had never started.
A haze squeezed my head, so I remained
unaware. He
     sat   rigid;
I noticed
that despair
suddenly filled
my stomach,
but
there were too many smells, silence, and stale air to taste it.

Analysis

A

Brown hair, dark eyes, a sensual
authority to each step, each movement:
she sunk on hands and knees
to propose new stretches, and
your eyes were mouths, salivating
for just a taste.

B

She sat neatly on the boat seat,
a hard
apple cider between her
legs.
You sat with your feet
splayed out,
and what was between
your legs
was hard.

C

"She is
my type." My engagement
ring
began to boil, red
rubies, like the blood
for which it is
named.

Synthesis

I am bony, freckled, covered
in light-blonde hairs, covered
in thick anxiety,

and, no matter how hard
I worked, I never turned you
on.

The pink scar

on Ruby's lips etched
her smile higher into her cheeks. I was gone,
just down the road, finishing the drive
from Manassas. A Wednesday, in the middle
of so many tasks and daily challenges
I had been prepared to complete,
but the microwave cord was one I forgot.

Her red coat was flat and sticky
with foaming drool. White socked paws
did not quiver, did not twitch, did not move.
The amber of her eyes sunk, as if they were
drowning in the surrounding white.

IS SHE DEAD? I couldn't see
the answer between
the tears, the anger. He stood at the top
of the basement stairs, still wiping the grease
around his stained hands with a used white sock.
It was an action
with no result.

Her name did not return
her consciousness; she lay
with an infantile heartbeat in my arms
as he drove, unphased, to the animal hospital.
Oddly, it had just snowed,
yet the afternoon's icy
picture was only Ruby's eyes
and the pink rupture alongside her mouth.

Little did I know that this would not
be the last puckering scar
to haunt me.

Are you my father-in-law?

Under-salted carrots, harsh
Merlot, firm potatoes, an evening
meal with Dr. Sexist and Mrs. spineless,
misery crowded the table. Vermont folk
gurgled through tattered speakers; "I have drunk
Cognac with the great (*whatever the hell
his name is*), don't you know, but you sound
spoiled when you talk."
Oh.
Merlot, now backwash, and sharp rip-cutting
through overcooked steak. "I have seen
the biggest set on (*this poor soul*) at the hospital,
like wowza, and I tell my son
how small yours are, when you leave."
I know.
A course in dining
with a misogynist
taught me nothing
new about the world,
so I played pretty
for the hour

and waited
my turn.

I am very disciplined
at waiting.

Listen to Your Gut

Streptococcus,
staphylococcus, lactobacillus,
peptostreptococcus,
bacteroides,
penicillium, rhodotorula

adorn the posy:
my microbial gut flora display.
Bright plumes of fungi and yeast, bacteria
and archaea demanding
attention, wrapped in delicate ribbons,
and vased tactfully.
Biochemical signaling
to the central nervous system: forget me

not,
listen to me
not,
stomach
in knots.
Clostridium,
faecalibacterium,
eubacterium, ruminococcus,
bifidobacterium

are efflorescent blossoms along
my gastrointestinal tract. Full
of answers, filaments of wisdom, insight,
and instinct.
Will you
marry me? An imploration,

a demand, an abuse.
Dendrites flare in warning; Belladonna
peek through the carnations' aurora.
Yes, a question, a doubt,
a misgiving which withers my bouquet, pulls in
its graceful sepals, and laces my gut
with resentment.

August 26th, 2017; 10:00 AM

Brought to my knees, a sharp
crack. An old wound split
open. Gasping, trying to keep up
with the movement, my mind employed
chess's strategic analysis. Were you one step
ahead? Bobby Fischer maneuvered
my hands,
my heart.

Wrapped in your thick, scarred arms,
not unlike an embrace
of adoration or desire,
arms gripping with frightening strength,
my ribs and back throbbed
with an exhaustion,
a fight which I lived
for eternity.
I grabbed
the knife.
I grabbed
the knife.
The knife

was in my hand,
but I had no idea what to do.
So, you felled me, and my stomach
bruised against the floor of the laundry
room. It was in my hand; I held
the knife, yet you held my hand.

You grasped my fingers
under yours.
Expertly. You held
my hand which held the knife,
and your-my hand stabbed me.
You idolized killers, you idolized torn

characters; you tore
my neck, idolizing killing me.

I bled and crawled; I bled and pulled;
I bled and bled.

Hungry pleas and begging for whys
and hows, for help, for 911,
for my Mommy
gurgled up with each hiccup of blood.
In the arms of a madman,
in my home, surrounded by walls which I had painted
with cool gray, honey yellow, and small dreams
of starting a family, I saw
my death, so a hot vengeance climbed my spine.

I bled and pushed; I bled and
fought. I bled and bled.

You tired of my fight, so you wedged
my bleeding neck into the crook of your elbow
and sought the finality of my last inhale.
As your grip grew,
Mississippis passed by,
my eyesight began to divide into particles
of light and dark, I held onto
my breath
and gave it to myself
as a gift, a parting gift, a small farewell
to life. I took my breath-

Even in the Dark

In
an empty space
the black
Are these memories mine?
I think
I don't think
My name: a picture that I will
recognize
once this ends
I feel warm
warm nothingness
and nothingness feels
me, holds me, suspends me through
the moments
that I can't consciously count now
I'm not alive,
am I? When will I know?
My eyes are all that is left to me
and I can close them
as my air runs out
my body is there
in the laundry room
but I am here
in the black
in the nothingness
Where will I hide
so he can't find me?
he can't take life from me again
And if he stabs me again
if he chokes me again
if he slams me onto the defiled linoleum
and digs his fingers into my throat again
I will be here, away,
hidden, safe,
unfeeling
in the black

until the EMT woke me up.

Nine Lives: A Question

To consider everyone's attendance
during my incident, the whereabouts
of my two feline housemates
comes into question.

Perhaps,
pushed to the basement
by my shrieks and pleas, they quietly braced
their quivering frames against
one another.

Perhaps,
drawn by the smell
of fresh blood, they paced hungrily
along the edge
of the dog-chewed rug.

Perhaps,
sitting patiently
by the kitchen, they conjured
a spell, like the mystic familiars
of their ancestry. Whiskers touching,
eyes midnight with dark magic, they forged
a new life, a cat-life, one of their nine
lives, and they blessed it onto
my broken body.

Perhaps,
I have the spirited grace
and luck of feline fortitude,
by which Death
is so easily eluded.

Perhaps,
I shouldn't question it
because curiosity killed
the cat,
you know.

ICU

Parasympathetic nervous system

Deep breaths fill
the life I have been granted.

Sympathetic nervous system

Gagging on the balloon in my throat, holding
my esophagus open and the stitches
steady.

Parasympathetic nervous system

Mom caresses my right hand, kissing
my scratched knuckles.

Sympathetic nervous system

Blinding white
in my frontal lobe, a migraine. Sight
is replaced with the watery haze
from a desert road.

Parasympathetic nervous system

The doe-like nurse washes the congealed
blood from my tangled hair.

Sympathetic nervous system

I need to rip the feeding tube
out of my nose, to tear off the sensors,
and pluck my blood-burst eyes
from my skull.

The main floor room

is my skin
inside out
and trapping me
within.

The hiss of *visceral*
is the machine standing behind
my left ear.

Each artery pulse reverberates
through the vermillion walls,
suspending me in perpetual
fear.

My Practice of "Past Self" in the Corner Room

was to ensure that everyone else present
didn't feel threatened by the torture
in my brain, body, and soul.
How long have you been a smoker?
the nurse pushed the stethoscope's cold
diaphragm against my bruised back
and listened to the volcanic gurgle
of loose blood in my lungs. Her question
was completely remote from reality. A thoughtless
shaking of my head, resulting in an unexpected pull
on the nasal feeding tube, regurgitated me
from the odd fantasy of being relocated
in the Step Down Unit for smoking, not—this.
So, I simply winced in place of answering.

Cradling my father's sinewy, freckled arm,
which once had effortlessly carried
my newborn frame, we paced
small circles, like two wingless bees
trying to remember the ease of flight. Around
the Nurses' Station with the overextended healthcare
workers,
much younger than I—and I had just turned 28—
I held my gown's chest pocket
which wished to swing wide,
burdened with the tangled wires
from four chest sensors, a wound drainage collector,
and the clamped end of the exhausting feeding tube.
Let's go look at the trains.
Matching my weak stride, he made it an easy shuffle
down the ramp
to the mainly window-lit corridor
and the stock photos
of trains.

mybrainhurts
I remember everything that happened
IAMGOINGTOTHROWUP

Gripping his arm and not allowing
the bloating sensation in my head to monopolize,
I noted how the trains neatly rounded
the rocky cliffs with scenic autumnal leaves
and thick West Coast river water
encompassing the journey. Childlike guesses
were made as to the location of the fantasy
illustrated. *Maybe one day,*
we can go on a train in Colorado.
The trains were seconds away
from entering
a yawning tunnel. Nodding,

bile blood bile blood bile blood
choking
My eyes ache; they dilate, then retract.
whathappened
Stop thinking.

I let myself ask to return to the Corner Room.
The ramp, now an incline, posed some challenge
for the hospital socks, but, soon,
my warm, reserved father eased me
back into the pleather chair.
The volcanic rust-phlegm swelled in my mouth,
stuffing my cheeks, and, with the only tube I was grateful
to attach to my body, I alleviated
the brimming with a MacGyvered vacuum.
Twenty-two-year-old Nurse Jennifer appeared and asked
to plug-in my feeding tube and sensors.

Above, the mounted wall-clock
had made an eight-minute adjustment
in its projection of time.

I stood for another walk.

The Barium Swallow Test

Sickly-green light sent shadows across
the sheet, and the bloated veins
paraded under the skin. Hands, not knowing
whether to grip the fabric in pathetic fear
or to defensively lay lifeless, performed a quiet dance
until a budding sense of lunacy, a question about reality
gnawed at the neocortex and salivated
over the thalamus. Sweet medicinal air-conditioning
flowed over chest and neck; prickly
goosebumps engorged the flesh.

The sun does not move in concrete walls; hours may have
evaporated, as the only ticking of time was left
to the ragged breathing of the form in the second bed.

A tech, a Saturday-morning-cartoon replicate,
with crooked rectangular wired glasses, cliché coffee-stained
lab coat, and a haphazard arrangement of moles
shook the metal frame and rolled the socked feet side-to-side.
Pushed out of the holding area and into the hallway, the bed
was a shopping cart under a wild twelve-year-old seeking
substance-less Pop-tarts. The wheels skipped
as the transporting platform scuffed every corner turned. Released from
his grip, the cart-bed rolled into the lab, only to stop
with the most important rule of physics: collision.

The room emptied with no direction. Shifting the starchy sheet back,
terry clothed heels wavered on the polished linoleum. Gown draped
over shoulders which had once been thrown onto a floor
like this. Aches lingered in soft tissues,
and, seemingly, they would never expire.
A cup, a paper water-fountain cup, lodged against
torture marred nose
with

the steamy pungency of newly laid
Virginia Beach hot asphalt, spilled gasoline
on the 1988 lawn mower, opossum
innards plastered on the yellow parallels by a roaming van.

Instructions to stand behind innocuous panels; a disappearing
act perhaps, but the buzz of equipment offset
invisibility. So, the hands gave the cup to the mouth
which gave the fluid-rot to the throat that held
it in a small pool for infinite seconds.
A gag, and inflammation rocketed specks
into the nasal cavity. (Please remember that the splinter
of the sinus will disrupt drinking routines
for the next 3 years.)

The tech checked his watch.

Hands gave mouth the cup again; molten plastic serpentined
into esophagus, and the click of machine confirmed
that the electromagnetic radiation seized corrupted evidence.
The tech rushed to the x-ray and demanded
a safety pin.

The pin closed off vulnerability
within the cavernous gown, vanished
breasts, secreted femininity;
it kept the murderous masculine toxicity at bay.
Purple fingers with glued cuts unlatched
its armor, and the venomous draft groped
the neck and chest and sternum and waist.
Gripped in hand, the pin pressed protection
into broken calluses.

The panels met gaze with new hunger and grabbed
drifting body, peeled back surgery-slick derma, seized
bruised rib cage, fingered epiglottal, and traced
the mortality
all
the
way
down.

Obituary

There is a cafe, two blocks away, home to
the dead and dying. Collecting around
tepid cups of coffee, *no sugar thanks,*
to disclose those last precious moments
of life and suffering, pain and relief.

His mustache catches beads of condensation
from the rim of yellowed porcelain. *It hit
around midnight.* His wife nods.
The heart attack? The neighboring booth
leans in, frail breaths fall from cigar-lungs.
My arm didn't even light up, he admits and guffaws.

They rest in chairs farthest from the door, veiled
in the rising October sunlight. The space
between is voided by the aloof, restless families
seeking breakfast in their ordinary routine.

But I can hear them: the dead. My voice
can't travel to them. Yet, left agape,
a weak wrinkle in the shroud remains
open for me.

Her hair refuses to lay flat, morning finds
the starchy hairspray, and the nose pieces
of her cat-eye glasses tangle in retreating strands
of her archaic bangs. *My daughter found me,
in bed, but that's where I always was.*
Her coffee shines
with cream. *She could have at least
fed the cat before coming upstairs.*

I hear old age and weathered-lives repeat
in their stories; there was never a chair
ready for me. Two days after
my 28th birthday, I was pulled
into the dark tunnel of asphyxiation. My heart
did not stop, nor did my breathing, but
the opening to the world beyond
was given to me, on me,
through me,
through my neck.

I sip my coffee and feel the remnants of death
slide down my throat.

Afterlife

Inside the ambulance
is where I remain. Each new morning
lays me back on the rickety gurney.
Today's date? His mustache locks
my swimming eyes, a dizziness increasing
from the loss of blood.

It's today.

The ceiling, punched by the fan's steady
shadow, stares back.

Yesterday

I forgot
my phone at home, and I lost
my name and the court file
attached to it. There wasn't a CD peeking out
of the red folder's pocket,
labeled
PHOTOS AUGUST 26 2017.
My lawyers smiled and waved
to each other
in the halls
of the Victim Witness Protection office, neither one
holding the plea deal
the criminal aggravatingly manipulated.
The Commonwealth Attorney,
whose daughter I attended
high school with, didn't see me
on the street
and gingerly ask how I am doing.

These things didn't happen,
oddly dissipating
from history, in the night
that I drank too much
cheap champagne, and left my empty purse
to dangle on the plastic wedding chair,
and danced independently.
Someone asked me why
I did this alone, several feet away
from the crowd; I pretended
to not hear her.

But that torturous acronym sauntered
out of another's lips: *PTSD*.
My drink became stale
as it writhed
along the internal ridge of my scar.
The months of waiting for the trial
slammed back into my yesterdays;
the eight years of the imprisoned person
and my perfect liberty
recoiled to five. Three years of healing
returned to one exhaustive, debilitative anticipation.

Looking Glass

Sometimes,
I catch myself, staring
in, from outside, through
the glass door as if it is a pane
of a fish tank. I watch
the participants inside
swim easily
behind
the transparent border.
It's a community of creatures, effortlessly
spending time
together.
The biggest space
is filled with memories.
They too swim up
and press their ugly faces to the glass.

Mackenzie Rose is a survivor. On August 26, 2017, only two days after her 28th birthday, the man with whom she shared a home plunged a chef's knife into her throat, past her tongue, and through the roof of her mouth. After eight days of recovery in the hospital, Mackenzie re-entered the world with a limited ability to speak, a PEG feeding tube, and PTSD (post-traumatic stress disorder). After relentless therapies, she began to reclaim some semblance of normality and retrained her voice to carry her new narrative. Mackenzie is a professor of Communications and English at Shenandoah University and a PhD student of trauma studies at Virginia Polytechnic Institute and State University. She can be found speaking at public functions about destigmatizing trauma.

With her dog, Bertie, Mackenzie Rose frequently escapes to the beautiful wilderness of the Shenandoah National Park to recharge and find peace in Nature's healing qualities.

For more information, please visit *rosestorytelling.com*.

www.ingramcontent.com/pod-product-compliance
Lightning Source LLC
Chambersburg PA
CBHW022053080426
42734CB00009B/1324